YOUR TWENTY-FIRST CENTURY PRAYER LIFE

The Poiema Poetry Series

Poems are windows into worlds; windows into beauty, goodness, and truth; windows into understandings that won't twist themselves into tidy dogmatic statements; windows into experiences. We can do more than merely peer into such windows; with a little effort we can fling open the casements, and leap over the sills into the heart of these worlds. We are also led into familiar places of hurt, confusion, and disappointment, but we arrive in the poet's company. Poetry is a partnership between poet and reader, seeking together to gain something of value—to get at something important.

Ephesians 2:10 says, "We are God's workmanship . . ." *poiema* in Greek—the thing that has been made, the masterpiece, the poem. The Poiema Poetry Series presents the work of gifted poets who take Christian faith seriously, and demonstrate in whose image we have been made through their creativity and craftsmanship.

These poets are recent participants in the ancient tradition of David, Asaph, Isaiah, and John the Revelator. The thread can be followed through the centuries—through the diverse poetic visions of Dante, Bernard of Clairvaux, Donne, Herbert, Milton, Hopkins, Eliot, R. S. Thomas, and Denise Levertov—down to the poet whose work is in your hand. With the selection of this volume you are entering this enduring tradition, and as a reader contributing to it.

—D.S. Martin
Series Editor

Your Twenty-First Century Prayer Life

Poems

NATHANIEL LEE HANSEN

CASCADE *Books* · Eugene, Oregon

YOUR TWENTY-FIRST CENTURY PRAYER LIFE
Poems

The Poiema Poetry Series

Cascade Books
An Imprint of Wipf and Stock Publishers
199 W. 8th Ave., Suite 3
Eugene, OR 97401

www.wipfandstock.com

PAPERBACK ISBN: 978-1-5326-4113-8
HARDCOVER ISBN: 978-1-5326-4114-5
EBOOK ISBN: 978-1-5326-4115-2

Cataloguing-in-Publication data:

Names: Hansen, Nathaniel Lee, author.

Title: Your twenty-first century prayer life : poems / Nathaniel Lee Hansen.

Description: Eugene, OR: Cascade Books, 2018 | The Poiema Poetry Series.

Identifiers: ISBN 978-1-5326-4113-8 (paperback) | ISBN 978-1-5326-4114-5 (hardcover) | ISBN 978-1-5326-4115-2 (ebook)

Subjects: LCSH: American poetry—21st century.

Manufactured in the U.S.A.   01/05/18

Amy

Contents

I.

Your Twenty–First Century Prayer Life

Your most frequent requests:
300 safe interstate miles,
night of sufficient sleep, a liner
sturdy for the class's ocean.
Names you speak again, again—
bless Andrew, bless Lynne.

You wonder how saints
master discipline, currents
of communication in crackling
lines, sparking from sender
to receiver, back again.

You can count on one hand
when prayer blossomed
organically without desire's
weeds crowding petals,
stealing sunlight, robbing
soil of water and life.

Your petitions persist,
abundant (overflowing)
with *me, my,* and *I.*
You forget, if you want
to live you must lose
your life.

Some Sundays You Consider Leaping from the Ship of Church

I.

No faith crisis,
no desire for licentiousness
(no prospects for an affair),
no compulsion for the NFL.

Rather the cardinal's song,
the wren's coloratura,
the mockingbird's imitative chirp,
the mourning dove's childlike coo.

To lay in bed, listen—
wouldn't that be sufficient?
Who needs the dressing up
of clothes, of disposition?

II.

Church bell marks eight o'clock,
harkening to monks' measured days,
time for measured prayer.
It interrupts your slothfulness.

You ready yourself with wrinkled shirt,
khakis, and hope—your wife
and two kids waiting for you
and your faith at the threshold.

Reading Scripture

You approach with suspicion yanking
on his leash, sniffing everywhere—
disbelief already dropped at the shelter
(though you haven't finalized papers).

You expect words will admonish:
deeds you didn't know you've done;
deeds you've done that you know well.
No matter your hiding, you will be rescued.

Bad Sermons

You've suffered your share. The worst
aren't the predictable and cheap,
forgettable as newsprint—noble attempts
at the Trinity; ignoble attempts
to discredit evolution in twenty minutes;
bellowing about non-essentials as if they
equal Christ's body and blood.

1. A minister confesses that he lacks
a poetic bone (reason to be scared).
Solomon read as Christ. The lover's
"dark skin" evidence of her sin.
He ignores the obviously erotic.
You and your wife scribble notes
screaming out ridiculous exegesis.

2. A minister diverges from Scripture,
eulogizing a recently deceased
politician (the man self-admittedly not
a Christian). Disbelief, more than anger,
drenches you that fall morning.
(The latter arrives later). Never
have you seen your wife so angry.

These wolves materialize
while you count sheep.
You jerk awake, afraid
and furious, pray for those
lambs—that they didn't swallow
lies as truths, that sharp teeth
didn't tear tender flesh.

Prayer Diagnostics

Your trouble is beginning—
so many activities more alluring.

You've never regretted prayer
(once you've finally started).

Others in your church life gush,
sincerely, about *prayer times*.

These people discomfort, fascinate.
You can't imagine yourself drenched.

And yet (and yet), you are jealous,
desiring what you don't possess.

They did not create their pools
of deep communion by themselves

with water already PH-balanced,
and free of bugs, branches, leaves.

But rather, steady labor of years—
much digging, much dirt to move.

It all returns to work of hands.

Hospitality

in Memoriam, Charlotte M. Hill (1926–2012)

I.

When Mom called, crying
you were in hospice,
it was as I expected
and hoped, for I wanted
your suffering to end, your body
already wracked beyond
medications' or surgery's
extensive but finite reach.

II.

Later when I spoke with you
(after Mom said you couldn't),
you did just that—words your way
of showing love, conversation
your gift, now however strained.
You said I made you proud.
I said, *I love you.* You said the same.

III.

I imagine you serving at the table
of the Lord. Though none will lack
anything, you'll still ask everyone
(once, twice, three times) if they
have enough—not that you lack faith—
but because you want all
to hunger and thirst no more.

Prayer ex Nihilo

I cannot make a thing
from nothing as you did.
I make from what you formed
to shape a work my own.

My prayers—pleadings, moans,
cries, whispers—sounds you thought
possible. Others grow
from models you planted.

Forgive my debts assumes
I've torn papers to bits.
*Your kingdom come, Your will
be done*—dicey endeavors.

That prayer declared as church:
vulnerability—
required for restoration,
genuine community.

First Things

You rise early, two hours before light,
house dormant, furnace set low.
You're between night and day,
coffee pot sputtering Sumatra's scent
to you kneeling, elbows on end table—
prayer the way you open your morning,
let your mind unpack before today's tasks.

Your elbows smart, bone against old wood
aches, but wakes you. Your hamstrings tire,
but you work through scribbled petitions,
some fresh, others you fear might be stale.

You've uttered them months and years,
questioning their efficacy,
your diligence, recalling Jesus
commending that persistent neighbor—
all that knocking on a door.

You are hoping names you've written
so many times along measured lines
will be written in one book
that can withstand elements, can resist
attempts to deconstruct or misconstrue.

Immobility

for J.C.

I.

You dropped your phone—a violent *smack* on the floor.
Some news electrocuted you—announcement of death.

You leaped from your chair as from a copperhead strike.
No way! you shook your head. A bite from death.

You rushed from the room as from a fire
only you could detect, consuming the body of life.

II.

Forgive me. One retrieved flung keys, another held you
while you gasped—hooked and landed, out of water.

Forgive me. Standing, I wanted to move, but unable
to will toward any purpose, my life with death minimal.

Forgive my standing, doing nothing. A sad truth—
I tend to halt and stare.

II.

The Canon

You've read it beginning to end five,
maybe six, times. Twice you did it in a year.
Each time your feet pulled down
in the same places, by usual suspects:
Numbers, Deuteronomy, Chronicles,
Revelation—all like quicksand.

You scramble up the rocks
of familiar places: *some* of Paul's letters,
James, Genesis, Psalms, the Gospels.
You cannot ignore the connections
stitched throughout the whole, connections
so numerous with yourself.

Praying in Your Office

With two young children,
you lack solitude.
Before sun, colleagues,
and students arrive,
you uncover it.

Close your calendar,
Abstain from email,
Power off your phone.
Focus on clock's tick.

Even with these efforts,
with all that stillness,
you're still
               distracted
as in a mall, signs
demanding your attention,
your fickle affections,
your weakened will.

Preschool Theology

The day it happens, you're shaving
three-day whiskers. Your son strolls in
and proclaims the Gospel: *Jesus died*
to pay the penalty for our sins
so we could be with God forever.

Razor in hand, you pause before
the next pull, consider that blood spilled
centuries ago, and all the blood spilled
centuries before that. *You're right*, you say,
checking your face for nicks, but finding none.

Decreasing Heat

How has so much of your on-fire
certainty cooled despite your tossing
on more kindling, another slab of cedar?

Surely you're failing your divine pursuit,
believing the heresy that passion
is the logical outcome of faith.

What of the dark night of the soul?
What of wrestling questions into a chokehold
only to have your grip pried away?

Like Peter, you say, *Lord, to whom should we go?*
You return to his words, contemplating
Pascal's wager, the bet of all bets.

You are not, by nature, a betting man.
You are stingy with your meager wealth.
You are left with your hand, the dealer

asking what you will do, your family and friends
watching to see if you'll slide those stacked chips
for everything buried in that green field.

Adhering Plastic Film on Window Frames

Before you seal those drafts, you pause
at one sill, invite the autumn pneuma.

An open book flusters in sudden air.
Summer's dust stirs one final time.

This rushing trips the thermostat—
you switch it off, yank down your sleeves.

This rearranging—openness
before the silence, before waiting

through that dry gap of centuries
between the testaments—a way

of enduring this last stretch of gray.

Poem as Prayer as Poem

Attempting the impossible
you arrange words to reach hearts—
yours and your audience's.

Best by yourself without others'
silent critiques, even your
own editorializing threatens you.

You trust the value of the oral, the aural
making meaning—route to sense
through well-selected sounds.

But you silence yourself and listen,
an act against your predisposition—
a fearful necessity.

Form and content matter, but not
as much as the posture of the heart.

Before the Season of Waiting is Waiting

That time of year when fields are gleaned but snow
has not descended—ugly weeks 'til Advent.

Colors that lit up fall? They're bagged or burnt.
Smoke cannot choke your impatience.

Restlessness interrupts your prayers. You wish
for one more candle each week, until four surround

the final white candle of descent, of the hope
of nations, prophecies fulfilled. Not yet.

Methods of Prayer

Sometimes it's best when you sit
and say nothing, pray nothing, be still.
This contradicts much you've absorbed
about prayer, against your will.

You learned the *Yes, Jesus* tag
to affirm others' prayers. It's rare
for you to mutter it, shyness shuts
your mouth, reservedness cuts off air.

You return to silence again,
needing earplugs to shut out
all noise. Oh, to be alone,
to be still, to subdue doubt.

The First Sunday of Advent in Central Texas

Memories of shoveling snow pile up
as you wear shorts and t-shirt,
your highly favored wardrobe.

It's 75 like a June day
from your Minnesota childhood,
leaves here green as those of memory.

A southerly bounces these leaves
that contemplate color shifts
they cannot hope to achieve.

You suspect this weather
resembles better that first Advent.
You light the first purple candle. Wait.

Praying in Your Car

I.

Starting as a way to cope with loss,
through the labyrinth of county
roads and within harmonies on mournful songs,
you offered your heart, pleaded for peace.

II.

During your morning commutes
you found yourself switching off music.
While other vehicles drove beside, in front, or behind,
you confessed, you repented, you requested.

III.

You pray aloud less often, preferring hum
of interstate, radial drone of wheels,
air rushing by tightly sealed tinted glass,
pine tree air freshener the holy incense.
Gas pedal pressed hard.
Thousands of RPMs towards the divine.

III.

Questions on Prayer

Do my words burst
like birdshot, scattered
throughout my day?
Do they pierce
your auricular feathers?

Or is my .22 a tool
best kept locked in a safe
whose combination is another's
favorite Bible verse?

Would you prefer the stones
I've unearthed each spring
hauled on a flatbed, neatly
piled in the North Forty's corner?

Are my words ruts
in township roads
that smoothly grid
tiled fields unable
to tame your works?

Would you prefer rocks skipped
across the lake of your vastness,
concentric circles my pleas,
my supplications, my praise?

You are dust, and unto dust you shall return

You feared those words
smeared across your forehead
each winter.

At the rail you submitted
to a blackened reminder—
your body's not forever.

Remnants of Palm Sunday
branches, ashes always
damper than you expected—
eternity in crossbeams.

Lenten Discipline (I)

You complied when Mom suggested *candy*
since there wasn't anything
as a kid you'd choose to be denied,
unless Valentine's Day fell during Lent.
If so, your stash waited
gathering fridge-top dust.

Your forehead marked with dust-
colored ash. Without candy,
for forty-plus days you waited,
not anxious, your motivations nothing
close to self-punishment then, Lent
something you wouldn't have denied.

Years since, you've varied your denials.
Soda once. All added sugar once. *You are dust*
and unto dust you shall return—Lent's
refrain atop your memory, like candy
atop that refrigerator. Anything
you fasted from a test of waiting,

seeing how long you can last. Waiting
never drew you toward God, your denials
rather a worship of your real god—not a thing—
but an eating disorder with binges. *Eat dust-*
tasting foods as punishment! (for sneaking candy,
picking through trash—not only in Lent.)

This year, you couldn't abstain during Lent,
exhausted from last year when you waited
forty days for sugar, even bland candy,
dark chocolate squares. Your denial
of sugars made other foods taste of dust,
appropriate penance for past binges. Anything

could be a binge—whether a thing
tasted pleasant didn't matter. Lent
had become a season of dust
on your love of God, of others, waiting
for your waistline to lessen, denying
your condition, like denying candy.

Anything better than living in misery of waiting
through Lent, under the disorder's hand, denied
moderation. Dust on candy jar, dust on hope.

Stations of the Cross

Your winter boots shuffled
through February and March
with your Wednesday-night class
around a cavernous church.

You studied a narrative, sculpted
in paling plaster, mounted
on winter-cold walls.

Each station adding more sorrow,
heavy as beams *you* shouldered—
you were forced to confess
only death could remake you.

Lenten Discipline (II)

One week in you reconsidered
a fast from sweet things.
Your children savored their Neapolitan,
each flavor troubling you.

A fast from sweet things
tormented you as you sat with them.
Each flavor troubled you.
You sipped your red wine, imagined.

It was a torment to sit with them.
You contemplated ceasing the fast.
You sipped your red wine, imagined
drinking a chocolate shake.

You contemplated ceasing the fast.
Warm days triggered fantasies of ice cream—
drinking a chocolate shake
from an oversized wine glass.

Warm days triggered fantasies of ice cream
especially after a sunny, hard run.
From an oversized wine glass,
you sipped, having survived seven days.

Especially after a sunny, hard run
you regretted committing to this fast.
You sipped. You survived seven days—
closer to forty days when you could celebrate.

You regretted committing to this fast,
your children savoring their Neapolitan.
Closer to forty days when you could celebrate,
one week in you were reconsidering.

Praying Hands

Fingers
hooked. Or fence posts
keeping out distractions.
Maybe makeshift bowls.
Position matters.

March Morning as Impetus for Prayer

Warped wooden door barricades distractions,

window cracked to morning's rainy reach,

screen's miniature squares graph-paper overcast sky,

pecan tree branches shadow soggy grass,

window-blind cord awaits prayer beads,

trance-inducing clock slows the heartrate,

desk lamp's glow candle-light in church—

Lord Jesus Christ, Son of God,

have mercy on me, a sinner.

American Evangelical Thought Crimes

Of Jesus's commands
Love your enemies is most
un-American, equal to a flag
upside down or scorched
with gasoline and shame.

Expect to be labeled *unpatriotic*,
accused of sympathy
for *those who would harm
our God-given land.*

(Never speak these thoughts
in your church's men's group.
Don't confess you've never
fired a gun, that you never
intend to start.)

Die daily to yourself?
Inconceivable
as turning the other cheek.

Lenten Discipline (III)

This was the year—you thought—when your fast
would top those of past years: no added sugar.
Even chocolate dressed itself in neglect.
For forty days, your oatmeal tasteless,
you convinced yourself this feat would help
you lose those extra pounds.
Those weeks you never contemplated God.
You made it all the way to Easter Sunday
thinking little of resurrection,
more about those cookies, frosting you had earned.
In Easter morning's shadow, your freedom gained,
you resumed your worship of confections
as if new covenants couldn't satisfy.

Golgotha

How to subvert
the violence of guilt
I've felt continually?

Do its fists batter
me as my deeds
have battered others?

Do their dreams
repeat scenes
I've acted in?

These possibilities
disrupt my rest,
my attempts to mollify.

Calcutta to Cannon Beach

That at times Mother Theresa
could not sense her Lord while sweating

words with pen read as a revelation
to me, disclosed her humanity.

God's omnipresence still too far—boils, sores,
and scars too near, so faith meant treading

waters of theology's raw mystery,
their paradox: belief is doubt

that we can know with certainty.
So I cup the ocean with my hands,

though fingers leak, dry, then crack.
For a moment, I can clutch the ocean

with my makeshift bowl, taste
salt my everyday eyes cannot see.

IV.

That First Easter (I)

No pyrotechnics
as with the burning bush.

No heavenly pronouncements
as at the transfiguration.

No disciples—they tossed
in hopeless sleep.

No legions of angels—
one or two dislocating stone.

Decorum

You pursue best line
breaks, metaphors, stanza
shapes, pin-point imagery.

You're never complacent
or naïve to commit
drafts to stone.

You prefer paper's
smooth portability.

Your mind corrals
lines for the night,
daily lets them roam.

Your prayers—tough
to tame—resist
domestication.

They rush counter
to your demands,
incessant requests.

They require freedom
that you fear offering.

You secure the gate
with a heavy-duty chain
any chance you get.

That First Easter (II)

Joy ravished me that sunrise
service, the hour I believed after years
in pews Sunday after Sunday.

Predictable scriptures through
which I'd nodded (groggy or wakeful)
now fresh as French-press coffee.

I couldn't sing hymns I'd heard
ad nauseam. A quickening surged
in my throat, my eyes—
the beautiful ache of belief.

Some days, it's all you can do not to pray

randomly. An hour earlier you were fine,
adjusted, even-keeled, then there was pressure
in your chest you had to answer.
There is no way to explain.
It doesn't happen often enough
to suggest a doctor's visit, but enough
to unsettle you for an afternoon or evening.

All you want is to be alone and pray:
in your car, in your bedroom, in your office.
Or best, in your backyard watching the feeder
where purple finches, cardinals, sparrows,
and white-tailed doves feast on sunflower seeds
before flying across the overgrown drainage basin.

That First Easter (III)

I.

From the time you rose in celebration,
her name was on your mind and lips.
The sermon's declaration lost on you,
another miracle impending.
At a friend's urging, you called her later
(already two dates down), not wasting
an hour with phone receiver wet
from sweat while you gained courage.

II.

She was beside you (finally) as you drove
out of town past fields ready for planting—
fifteen miles distant from light and deadlines—
to study what you'd always loved most: the sky.
You lay on gravel, close, but not touching.
You helped her navigate the shapes ancients
constructed, identifying as much as you could,
which wasn't much, but was enough.

Sunday Morning

for R.K. and B.K.

Listening to a sermon on prayer
you discover yourself distracted:
three rows in front, a father
holds his school-aged boy in his lap.

You discover yourself distracted,
study the smiles they share.
His school-aged boy in his lap,
the father beside the empty wheelchair.

You study the smiles they share,
watch the mother kiss their cheeks.
The father beside the empty wheelchair
he steers into the service each week.

Watching the mother kiss their cheeks,
you wonder how often they've pleaded.
He steers the boy into the service each week,
familiar aisle seat, should escape be needed.

You wonder how often they've pleaded
for immobility to end.
Familiar aisle seat—should escape be needed—
a part of their liturgy, a duty they tend.

For immobility to end
while the boy's breath rattles, limbs twitch—
a part of their liturgy, a duty they tend—
you're certain they've prayed for this.

While the boy's breath rattles, limbs twitch,
sometimes flail, parents strap him in his seat.
You're uncertain if they've prayed for this:
Could he one day move his feet?

Sometimes he flails; they strap him in his seat
and wheel him from the service to where?
Might he one day move his feet,
command his hands to move his chair?

They wheel him from the service to where—
a hallway, a room, outside?—you do not know.
Command your hands, move your chair—
these are givens. You go where you wish to go:

a hallway, a room, outside. You do not know
how they manage to keep their faith alive.
These are givens—you go where you wish to go.
You think little what it means to survive.

How do they manage to keep their faith alive?
Three rows in front, a mother and father.
You think little what it means to survive,
listening to a sermon on prayer.

On Your Son's Conversion

      I.

Your son has *prayed the prayer,*
your wife informs you via text,
says he wants to be a Christian,
and all you can think—beyond
thankfulness—is that you were gone
already, writing in your office.
So much to do, book review due
in a week, two weeks gone
since you finished the book.

      II.

You want to tell him sometimes
you're unsure. You want to tell him
it isn't *one* moment that's soon gone.
You want to tell him that faith
is a daily choice you make
like brushing teeth, bathing, dressing—
all bad examples, you know.
You want to teach him how to hang
onto red-lettered text just as he hangs
onto monkey bars, reaching from one
to the next, the distance below
enough to keep him moving forward.

By the Dawn's Early Light

In many American churches, it hangs
in a prominent position.

From its gaze we cannot hide—
its presence commands our devotion.

Unlike Lourdes or Fatima, no miracles
have been confirmed in our shrines.

These stripes (and stars) cannot heal,
cannot reconcile, though blood has been shed.

We know blood is required, as is *sacrifice*—
that word with its gory slipperiness.

On holy days in May and July, we sing anthems
and lavish extra allegiance. It still fails.

Farming in the Drought

Stalks of corn are browning from the ground up,
and soybeans, too, lose green this arid stretch.
An early spring led measured rows well past
knee-high by Fourth of July, yet growth spurts
might—in the end—be all for naught unless
this ever-cloudless sky delivers rain.

Temptation builds to question Providence
when daily prayers yield only stiffened knees.
In forty-seven years of farming corn and beans
you know you've never checked the forecast
this many times a day for changes
in this dying, desert-like environment
with its mirage of hanging-in-there green.

But then, come evening, some days hence,
while at the table figuring the loss
you stand to suffer, thunder trickles in
through windows shut to summer's reach.
You leave behind depressing numbers, run
outside to see lightning flash, to taste
the temperature descending sharply.
Wispy blue draped from nearing clouds
can only mean one thing: the word that in
your grateful, dumb state you cannot speak.

Prayerful Hydrology

At times, forcing a poem
is synonymous with forcing a prayer.
At such times, you wish you didn't care
so much about words' meanings, sounds.

How do you turn off that voice
that dams your attempted stream
of language aimed toward meaning,
aimed toward the divine?

How to rid water of branches,
of tree trunks, of fetid mud?
Oh, for a season of rain, of floods
to overpower all that is stagnant.

Oh, for loss of control that overpowers
everything in its path, that slows the hours.

Thanks

The Holy Trinity; Don Martin for reading and rereading this book and pushing me to keep sharpening it; Aaron Brown for offering suggestions on several of these poems; the University of Mary Hardin-Baylor for awarding me a summer research grant that enabled my work on this book; Mom and Dad for surrounding me with words and with love; Matthias and Estella for bringing me such joy; and Amy for, well, everything.

Acknowledgments

Category 2: Installment Two; Four Seasons West of the 95th Meridian: Farming in the Drought

The Cresset: Your Twenty-First Century Prayer Life, Prayerful Hydrology, Praying in Your Car

The Curator: Methods of Prayer

Between Midnight and Dawn: A Literary Guide to Prayer for Lent, Holy Week, and Eastertide; *The Passionate Transitory*: Calcutta to Cannon Beach

Perspectives: Prayer Diagnostics, Decreasing Heat

Saint Katherine Review: The Canon

COLLECTIONS IN THIS SERIES INCLUDE:

Six Sundays toward a Seventh by Sydney Lea

Epitaphs for the Journey by Paul Mariani

Within This Tree of Bones by Robert Siegel

Particular Scandals by Julie L. Moore

Gold by Barbara Crooker

A Word In My Mouth by Robert Cording

Say This Prayer into the Past by Paul J. Willis

Scape by Luci Shaw

Conspiracy of Light by D. S. Martin

Second Sky by Tania Runyan

Remembering Jesus by John Leax

What Cannot Be Fixed by Jill Peláez Baumgaertner

Still Working It Out by Brad Davis

The Hatching of the Heart by Margo Swiss

Collage of Seoul by Jae Newman

Twisted Shapes of Light by William Jolliff

These Intricacies by Dave Harrity

Where the Sky Opens by Laurie Klein

True, False, None of the Above by Marjorie Maddox

The Turning Aside anthology edited by D.S. Martin

Falter by Marjorie Stelmach

Phases by Mischa Willett

Second Bloom by Anya Krugovoy Silver

www.ingramcontent.com/pod-product-compliance
Lightning Source LLC
Chambersburg PA
CBHW032059040426
42449CB00007B/1140